EPIC

STUDY GUIDE

THE STORY GOD IS

JOHN ELDREDGE

with CRAIG MCCONNELL

Published by

THOMAS NELSON

Since 1798

www.thomasnelson.com

Published in Nashville, Tennessee, by Thomas Nelson, Inc.

Published in association with Yates & Yates, LLP, Attorneys and Counselors, Orange, California.

ISBN-10: 1-4185-0015-1
ISBN-13: 978-1-4185-0015-3

Printed in the United States of America.
07 08 09 10 — 9 8 7 6 5 4 3 2 1

CONTENTS

—◆—

INTRODUCTION

*I had always felt life first as a story—and if there is a story
there is a story teller.*

—G. K. CHESTERTON

This little study guide is offered to help you get the most out of the message of *Epic*. We're assuming that you are doing this as part of a group, perhaps in a class, a small group study, or a home fellowship. If you're going through this material alone, write out your answers to each of the questions as if you were "journaling" through your experience.

We recommend that you read the whole story of *Epic* before you start this study guide. After all, this about the Larger Story! You'll want to take it in before you explore it deeper.

Each week's session will present a couple of excerpts and several questions for you to answer prior to your group time. Each session will also encourage your to think through and write out *your story*. We'll also include some thoughts on the theology of each session, and the Scriptures referred to in the chapter being studied.

UTILIZING THE *EPIC DVD*

If possible, you may want to utilize the DVD presentation of the *Epic* material in conjunction with this study guide. This is a live presentation of the material by John Eldredge, and can really enhance your *Epic* experience. If you're doing this study in conjunction with your church, the DVD is available in the *Epic Church Kit*. You can also find *Epic DVD* in your local Christian bookstore or at www.thomasnelson.com.

If your group has access to this resource, we would suggest that you add a session on the front end of your group (making a total of seven sessions). Have your group gather, introduce one another and watch the 38-Minute Version on the *Epic DVD*, which is an introductory overview of the material by John. It will help everyone take in the whole story at once (which is usually the best way to take in a story). Follow up the viewing with a few simple interactive questions. A Facilitator's Guide is included with the DVD to help you make the most of your experience!

There is a Larger Story. And you have a crucial role to play.

INTRODUCTION

Ask the God of our Master, Jesus Christ, the God of glory—to make you intelligent and discerning in knowing him personally, your eyes focused and clear, so that you can see exactly what it is he is calling you to do, grasp the immensity of this glorious way of life he has for his followers, oh, the utter extravagance of his work in us who trust him— endless energy, boundless strength! (Ephesians 1:17–18 MSG)

PROLOGUE

Life, you'll notice, is a story.

Life doesn't come to us like a math problem. It comes to us the way that a story does, scene by scene. You wake up. What will happen next? You don't get to know—you have to enter in, take the journey as it comes. The sun might be shining. There might be a tornado outside. Your friends might call and invite you to go sailing. You might lose your job.

Life unfolds like a drama, doesn't it? Each day has a beginning and an end. There are all sorts of characters, all sorts of settings. A year goes by like a chapter from a novel. Sometimes it seems like a tragedy, sometimes a comedy. Mostly it feels like a soap opera. Whatever happens, it's a story through and through. And when it comes to figuring out this life you're living, you'd do well to know the rest of the story.

❧ *Have you viewed life, your life as an unfolding story? React to John's thought: "Life is a story."*

❧ *John shares the story about a father coming home to his daughter and a damaged car to make the point that if we don't know the full story, we can easily jump to the wrong conclusion. What conclusions have you jumped to regarding God and his heart towards you that may be the result of you not knowing the full story?*

Story is the language of the heart.

If you want to get to know someone, you need to know their story. Their life is a story. It, too, has a past and a future. It, too, unfolds in a series of scenes over the course of time. Why is Grandfather so silent? Why does he drink too much? Well, let me tell you. There was a terrible battle in World War II, in the South Pacific, on an island called Okinawa. Tens of thousands of American men died or were wounded there; some of them were your grandfather's best friends. He was there, too, and saw things he has never been able to forget.

✧ *How has hearing someone else's story changed the way you have looked at that person?*

We humans share these lingering questions: *Who am I really? Why am I here? Where will I find life? What does God want of me?* The answers to these questions seem to come only when we know the rest of the story.

❧ *How would looking at life as a great Story change the way you live? What questions might it answer for you? Does it affect your understanding of Christianity?*

WE HAVE LOST OUR STORY

If there is meaning to this life, then why do our days seem so random? What is this drama we've been dropped into the middle of? If there is a God, what sort of story is he telling here?

No wonder we keep losing heart. We find ourselves in the middle of a story that is sometimes wonderful, sometimes awful, often a confusing mixture of both, and we haven't a clue how to make sense of it all.

☙ *Can you relate to this confusion? What part of your story has caused you to lose heart?*

☙ *If our lives are a story, what kind of a story have you fallen into? Is it the kind of tale you have hoped for or dreamed of living? Why or why not?*

THERE IS A LARGER STORY

I want you to notice that all the great stories pretty much follow the same story line. Things were once good, then something awful happened, and now a great battle must be fought or a journey taken. At just the right moment (which feels like the last possible moment), a hero comes and sets things right, and life is found again.

All of these stories borrow from *the* Story. From Reality. We hear echoes of it through our lives. Some secret written on our hearts. A great battle to fight, and someone to fight for us. An adventure, something that requires everything we have, something to be shared with those we love and need.

There is a Story that we just can't seem to escape. There *is* a Story written on the human heart.

❖ *What would knowing the Larger Story explain about your life?*
What deep desires of your heart might the Larger Story explain?

Christianity, in its true form, tells us that there is an Author and that he is good, the essence of all that is good and beautiful and true, for he is the source of all these things. It tells us that he has set our hearts' longings within us, for he has made us to live in an Epic. It warns that the truth is always in danger of being twisted and corrupted and stolen from us because there is a Villain in the Story who hates our hearts and wants to destroy us. It calls us up into a Story that is truer and deeper than any other, and assures us that there we will find the meaning of our lives.

We won't begin to understand our lives, or what this so-called gospel is that Christianity speaks of, until we understand the Story in which we have found ourselves. For when you were born, you were born into an Epic that has already been under way for quite some time. It is a Story of beauty and intimacy and adventure, a Story of danger and loss and heroism and betrayal.

↩ *Have you ever thought of Christianity as an Epic Story in which you have a vital role? If this is a new thought, how have you viewed Christianity and your role in it previously?*

To have some clarity on the Larger Story would be gold right now, wouldn't it?

SOMETHING TO PONDER

❋ *What's your story? If you want to understand your own life, you must understand your story. The things that have happened in the past have shaped you into the person you are now. (The reason you have a fear of heights, the reason you move away from intimacy, all that). Over the next few weeks we're going to ask you to write out your story. This is huge. It will give you so much understanding of yourself, God's hand in your life, the enemy's assault on you, and of your role in God's Larger Story. So, begin to write it out below or tell it to someone. (Think about these things: How would you tell your story? What would you say and/or include? What's shaped you, made you who you are today?)*

THEOLOGY

In the Prologue, the idea is simply that life is a Story. That in fact Story is the nature of the world in which we live. This shouldn't be too startling, though it may come as a new idea to most people. Notice that the Bible is written primarily as stories, and that Jesus teaches primarily through stories (parables). The Gospels themselves are also *stories* about Jesus, which apparently is the best way to get to know him! As Eugene Peterson (who translated the version of the Scriptures called *The Message*) said, "We live in narrative, we live in story. Existence has a story shape to it. We have a beginning and an end, we have a plot, we have characters. The Scriptures are given to us in the form of a story."

✤ *Read Acts 1:1–3. Why do you think Luke needed to tell this story as a story?*

✦ *What would have been lost if he had simply listed some facts?*

Now, by using the concept of Story, John is not saying Christianity is untrue. Yes, there are teachers out there who try and reduce Christianity to "one of the world's great myths, or legends." That is not what John means. *Story* does not equal *untruth*. *Story* means, "a narrative account of unfolding events; a drama." And *epic* means, "a dramatic story on a grand scale."

Further, John is not saying that biblical truths cannot be stated as propositions. They can, and in many places in Scripture, they are. But historically speaking, the church has only recently fallen to the use of proposition as its *primary* means of communicating truth. That happened as a result of the modern era. (For a better understanding, read "Science and the Story That We Need" on www.epicreality.com). Proposition is important, but it is inadequate. The Bible reads far more like a great story than it does an encyclopedia, or the yellow pages.

Bottom Line: God has created a reality for mankind to live in, and that reality unfolds like a great story. And quite often, when God chooses to communicate with man, he does so through story (as in the many stories of the Old and New Testaments). Reality is a Story, and the best way to appreciate it, to understand it, is through story.

SUPPORTING SCRIPTURE

He has planted eternity in the human heart . . . (Ecclesiastes 3:11 NLT).

Act One

ETERNAL LOVE

*In the beginning was the Word, and the Word was with God,
and the Word was God. He was with God in the beginning.*

—JOHN 1:1–2 NIV

❧ *What is the apostle John describing in the verse above?*

❧ *What does this passage say about "the beginning" of the Story?*

❖ *And what does the passage say about God?*

❖ *For starters, what did this chapter in Epic stir up in you? New thoughts, questions, an "ah ha" moment?*

"In the beginning . . ." or "Once upon a time . . ."

It's a wonderful phrase, isn't it, full of legend and myth, promise and mystery, and a sort of *invitation*. "Come, let me show you something . . ."

Once upon a time there were a good king and queen who were very sad because they had no children. Once upon a time there was a beautiful maiden who lived with her wicked stepsisters. Once upon a time, of all good days of the year, on Christmas Eve. A long time ago, in a galaxy far, far away. All of the really good stories start that way.

And so, how does Act One of the Larger Story begin?

. . . in the ancient past there was a fellowship, a heroic intimacy, something called the Trinity.

❧ *Have you ever thought about what occupied God before he created the world? Did you picture him alone? What have you pictured God doing in eternity past (was it adventurous, exciting, or rather boring)?*

❧ *The Triune God is ultimately relational. Our origins are relational and thus we are relational . . . for we are created in his Image. What does it mean to say that we are relational?*

❧ *Would you describe yourself as relational? Would others?*

One of the deepest of all human longings is the longing to belong, to be a part of things, to be invited in. We want to be part of the fellowship.

❧ *How have you felt that longing in your life—both in your youth and today?*

❧ *Did you know that longing came from God?*

THE PROMISE OF ACT ONE

Something preceded us. Something good. We'd much rather be included in something grand than have to create the meaning of our lives. To know that life doesn't rest on our shoulders, but invites us up into it.

✤ *John shares the story of being invited up and into the unfolding story of his grandfather's world on a ranch in Eastern Oregon. Have you been chosen or invited into something like that—a great story or an adventure already in motion? If so, what was it?*

✤ *If not, what would you have liked to be invited into?*

❧ *One of the realities of a Larger Story is that Life is not all about you. You're precious, important, and valuable; you have a crucial role to play. But this story is about something bigger than you. Does that disturb, comfort, discourage, anger, or bring clarity to you?*

❧ *Have you thought of God as being part of your story this week? How?*

✦ *And have you thought of yourself as being part of God's story this week? How?*

SOMETHING TO PONDER

✦ *Continue to fill in the various seasons of your life with the good as well as the painful memories you've experienced through others. Include those times you were invited up and into some unfolding fellowship (or the times you wished you had been). Add these memories below to Your Story that you began to write last week.*

❧ *For those that journal, capture all that God is stirring in you through these first two sessions, the group discussion and your own quiet reflection. What is he saying to you through this?*

THEOLOGY

God is Trinity—Father, Son, and Holy Spirit. Thus, God is relational. (For further study on the theology of the Trinity, see Matthew 3:16–17, Matthew 28:19, John 15:26, 1 Peter 1:1–2.)

Every person longs to belong. We crave relationship, and we yearn to be invited into relationship—whether that's in a family, a group, a marriage, a church. That core human longing for relationship is evidence of what we are created for as image bearers of the God who is Trinity.

And God the Trinity longs to invite us into relationship with him. (See Jeremiah 24:7, John 17:3, 24.)

Finally, either we believe God is worthy to be the center of the Story and in him we'll find the life we're looking for, or we'll look for life somewhere else.

SUPPORTING SCRIPTURE

In the beginning was the Word, and the Word was with God, and the Word was God. He was with God in the beginning. Through him all things were made; without him nothing was made that has been made. (John 1:1-3 NIV)

In the beginning God created the heavens and the earth (Genesis 1:1 NIV).

Then God said, "Let us make man in our image . . ." (Genesis 1:26 NIV).

"Father, I want those you have given me to be with me where I am, and to see my glory, the glory you have given me because you loved me before the creation of the world." (John 17:24 NIV)

Life itself was in him (John 1:4 NLT)

Act Two

THE ENTRANCE OF EVIL

And there was war in heaven.
—REVELATION 12:7 NIV

✦ *As we turn the page into Act Two, let me ask you a question: Why does every story have a villain?*

Most people do not live as though our Story has a Villain, and that makes life very confusing. How have we missed this? All the stories we've been telling about the presence of an evil power in the world, all the dark characters that have sent chills down our spines and given us restless nights—they are spoken to us as *warnings*. There is evil cast around us.

◆ *Have you lived as though your story has a villain? How or why not?*

◆ *What questions does the reality of evil raise for you?*

On the twenty-fourth day of the first month, as I was standing on the bank of the great river, the Tigris, I looked up and there before me was a man dressed in linen, with a belt of the finest gold around his waist. His body was like chrysolite, his face like lightning, his eyes like flaming torches, his arms and legs like the gleam of burnished bronze, and his voice like the sound of a multitude. (Daniel 10:4–6 NIV)

We are not alone. This universe is inhabited by other beings; we share the stage with other players.

✧ *React to this reality. What does this stir up in you?*

The LORD sent an angel, who annihilated all the fighting men and the leaders and officers in the camp of the Assyrian king. (2 Chronicles 32:21 NIV)

The LORD sent a plague on Israel . . . and seventy thousand of the people from Dan to Beersheba died. When the angel stretched out his hand to destroy Jerusalem, the LORD was grieved because of the calamity and said to the angel who was afflicting the people, "Enough! Withdraw your hand." (2 Samuel 24:15–16 NIV)

Hold on, now. What sort of Epic is God telling here?

Why does he set the stage with winged creatures so beautiful and noble that we cannot look upon their faces without falling to our knees, so deadly that armies, cities, entire civilizations fall at the hands of a mere few? Yet there are "ten thousand times ten thousand" cast into this great Story (Daniel 7:10). What might it mean?

Perhaps this Story is not nearly as "safe" as we'd like to believe.

This is precisely what the Bible (and all the stories that echo it) has warned us about all these years: we live in two worlds—or in one world with two halves, part that we can see and part that we cannot. We are urged, for our own welfare, to act as though the unseen world (the rest of reality) is, in fact, more weighty and more real and more dangerous than the part of reality we can see.

❧ *Is that how you've lived your life?*

✛ *Is that how you see the world?*

. . . the Holocaust, child prostitution, terrorist bombings, genocidal governments. What is it going to take for us to take evil seriously?

Life is very confusing if you do not take into account that there is a Villain. That you, my friend, have an Enemy.

✛ *In the past, who have you blamed for the pain and sorrows of life?*

One of the things that surprised me when I first read the New Testament seriously was that it talked so much about a Dark Power in the universe—a mighty evil spirit who was held to be the Power behind death, disease, and sin . . . Christianity thinks this Dark Power was created by God, and was good when he was created, and went wrong. Christianity agrees . . . this is a universe at war. (C. S. Lewis, *Mere Christianity*)

❧ *How would you live differently if you believed this to be true?*

At the end of Act Two, Evil has entered the story in dreadful form, and God's own heart has been called into question.

Now the stage is set for Act Three.

SOMETHING TO PONDER

❧ *It seems there are two extremes when it comes to the devil. We either live as if he doesn't exist or we are so focused upon him that we see him behind every inconvenience. What extreme have you been more prone to?*

◦ *What in your life, your story, do you now understanding may very well have been the work of the villain? What has he tried to steal, kill, or destroy from you in the past? What is he currently assaulting you with (lies, accusation, shame, guilt, temptation, etc.)? What are you going to do about it?*

THEOLOGY

God created angelic beings (see Hebrews 1). One of them, Satan, betrayed God and led a revolt against Him (see Revelation 12). Defeated, Satan and his angelic allies were cast out of heaven. This foe of God is our adversary. Described as a thief, murderer, and destroyer (John 10:10), the accuser of the faithful (Revelation 12:10), the devil, he is no impotent imaginary character. Rather he is a present and real enemy who seeks only defamation, death, and destruction for believers. Unfortunately, for a variety of reasons, many believers do not take his existence or scriptural warnings and instructions about him seriously; thus, his activity is often attributed either to God or us. To live the life God has for us demands that we deal with our enemy.

There is a teaching circulating around the church right now which says we must *not* "fight back" or do anything to resist the devil—that such activity puts too much emphasis on Satan and should be left to God. This is very dangerous teaching and very unbiblical as well. In James 4:7 and in 1 Peter 5:8–9, we are *commanded* to resist Satan. In Ephesians 6:10–18 we are told to put on the armor of God because we will be doing battle against the enemy. Certainly we have Christ as our example, who dealt firmly and directly with foul spirits (see Mark 5:1–17, Luke 4:31–37). We also have the example of Paul in Acts 16:16–18.

A note of clarification: The "war in heaven" referred to in Revelation 12:7 clearly takes place in Act Three, at the time of

Christ's birth. It is not the same war John refers to taking place in Act Two. It is a biblical *example* of war between holy and unholy angels. Now, we know Satan must have fallen *prior* to Genesis 3, because at this point he is the enemy of God, looking to deceive and destroy Adam and Eve. Exactly how he fell, and when he fell, is not directly referred to in Scripture, but only through inferences such as in Ezekiel 28. This we know: Satan is now the enemy of God and God's people (Revelation 12:17, 1 Peter 5:8–9), he has many fallen angels in his army (Luke 8:26–31), and we are going to need to actively resist him (James 4:7 and 1 Peter 5:9).

SUPPORTING SCRIPTURE

"The thief comes only to steal and kill and destroy; I have come that they may have life, and have it to the full." (John 10:10 NIV)

And the LORD sent an angel, who annihilated all the fighting men and the leaders and officers in the camp of the Assyrian king. So he withdrew to his own land in disgrace. And when he went into the temple of his god, some of his sons cut him down with the sword. (2 Chronicles 32:21 NIV)

So the LORD sent a plague on Israel . . . and seventy thousand of the people from Dan to Beersheba died. When the angel stretched out his hand to destroy Jerusalem, the LORD was grieved because of the calamity and said to the angel who was afflicting the people, "Enough! Withdraw your hand." (2 Samuel 24:15–16 NIV)

*"Release the four angels who are bound at the great river Euphrates."
And the four angels who had been kept ready for this very hour and
day and month and year were released to kill a third of mankind.*
(Revelation 9:14–15 NIV)

*"You were the model of perfection, full of wisdom and perfect in
beauty.*

*You were in Eden, the garden of God; every precious stone
adorned you: ruby, topaz and emerald, chrysolite, onyx and jasper,
sapphire, turquoise and beryl. Your settings and mountings were made
of gold; on the day you were created they were prepared.*

*You were anointed as a guardian cherub, for so I ordained you.
You were on the holy mount of God; you walked among the fiery stones.*

*You were blameless in your ways from the day you were created
till wickedness was found in you."* (Ezekiel 28:12–15 NIV)

*"I drove you in disgrace from the mount of God, and I expelled you, O
guardian cherub, from among the fiery stones. Your heart became
proud on account of your beauty, and you corrupted your wisdom
because of your splendor."* (Ezekiel 28: 16–17 NIV)

*On the twenty-fourth day of the first month, as I was standing on the
bank of the great river, the Tigris, I looked up and there before me was
a man dressed in linen, with a belt of the finest gold around his waist.
His body was like chrysolite, his face like lightning, his eyes like flaming torches, his arms and legs like the gleam of burnished bronze, and*

his voice like the sound of a multitude. I, Daniel, was the only one who saw the vision; the men with me did not see it, but such terror overwhelmed them that they fled and hid themselves . . . I had no strength left, my face turned deathly pale and I was helpless. (Daniel 10:4–8 NIV)

Act Three

The Battle for the Heart

The thief comes only to steal and kill and destroy;
I have come that they might have life, and have it to the full.
—John 10:10 NIV

Act Three begins in darkness.

Darkness over the deep and God's breath hovering over the waters.
(Genesis 1:2 *Alter*)

Suddenly a voice breaks the silence, and there is light.

Another word is spoken, and the great canopy of the heavens is unfurled, a sky more blue than you've ever seen it, yet translucent when it is dark to reveal the stars that lie beyond.

Yet another word, and the seas draw back to reveal the land masses of earth.

Again a word, and mangoes laden the branches of their trees...

~ *What does John's description of Creation stir in you? Has the creation account, as you've heard or understood it before been rather dull, scientific, unromantic? How have you thought of Creation?*

Into this world God opens his hand, and the animals spring forth. Myriads of birds, in every shape and size and song, take wing—hawks, herons, warblers. All the creatures of the sea leap into it—whales, dolphins, fish of a thousand colors and designs. Thundering across the plains race immense herds of horses, gazelles, buffalo, running like the wind. It is more astonishing than we could possibly imagine. No wonder "the morning stars sang together and all the angels shouted for joy" (Job 38:7 NIV). A great hurrah goes up from the heavens!

We have grown dull toward this world in which we live; we have forgotten that it is not *normal* or *scientific* in any sense of the word. It is fantastic. It is fairy tale through and through. Really now. Elephants? Caterpillars? Snow? At what point did you lose your wonder at it all?

❧ *What in nature has taken your breath away this past year?*

Creation unfolds like a great work of art, a masterpiece in the making. And just as you can learn about an author by the stories he tells, you can learn a great deal about an artist from the works he creates. Surely you see that God is more creative than we can possibly imagine, and romantic to the core. Lovers and honeymooners choose places like Hawaii, the Bahamas, or Tuscany as a backdrop for their love. But whose idea was Hawaii, the Bahamas, or Tuscany?

Let's bring this a little closer to home. Whose idea was it to create the human form in such a way that a kiss could be so delicious? And he didn't stop there, as only lovers know.

❖ *Lingering in the thought of Creation, what does Eden tell you about God, his desire for man, and the life we were meant to live?*

I daresay we've heard a bit about original sin, but not nearly enough about original glory, which comes *before* sin and is deeper to our nature. We were crowned with glory and honor. Why does a woman long to be beautiful? Why does a man hope to be found brave? Because we remember, if only faintly, that we were once more than we are now.

God creates us in his image, with powers like unto his own—the ability to reason, to create, to share intimacy, to know joy. He gives us laughter and wonder and imagination.

❧ *Have you thought about "original glory" before?*

❧ *What does the idea stir in you?*

THE GREATEST DIGNITY OF ALL

He enables us to love.

He gives us the greatest treasure in all creation: a heart. For he intends that we should be his intimate allies, who join in the Sacred Circle of intimacy that is the core of the universe, to share in this great Romance.

Just as we have lost our wonder at the world around us, we have forgotten what a treasure the human heart is. All of the happiness we have ever known and all of the happiness we hope to find is unreachable without a heart. You could not live or love or laugh or cry had God not given you a heart.

And with that heart comes something that just staggers me.

God gives us the freedom to reject him.

He gives to each of us a will of our own.

⊷ *What is God hoping for by giving you a free will?*

So if you are writing a story where love is the meaning, where love is the highest and best of all, where love is the *point,* then you have to allow each person a choice. You have to allow freedom. You cannot force love. God gives us the dignity of freedom, to choose for or against him (and friends, to ignore him is to choose against him).

This is the reason for what Lewis called the Problem of Pain. Why would a kind and loving God create a world where evil is possible? Doesn't he care about our happiness? Isn't he good? Indeed, he does and he is. He cares so much for our happiness that he endows us with the capacity to love and to be loved, which is the greatest happiness of all.

He endows us with a dignity that is almost unimaginable.

∾ *Did you know that God gave man free will—to choose for him, choose to love? How does that shape you understanding of the "Problem of Pain"?*

↬ *To what or to whom have you given your heart in the past? To whom or to what have you most recently given it?*

PARADISE LOST

Evil was lurking in that Garden. The mighty angel had once been glorious as well, more glorious than we. He was, if you recall, captain of the Lord's armies, beautiful and powerful beyond compare. But he rebelled against his Creator, led a great battle against the forces of heaven, and was cast down. Banished but not destroyed, he waited in the shadows for an opportunity to take his revenge.

You must understand: the Evil One hates God, hates anything that reminds him of the glory of God . . . wherever it exists. Unable to overthrow the Mighty One, he turned his sights on those who bore his image.

Satan came into the Garden and whispered to Adam and Eve—and in them, to all of us—"You cannot trust the heart of God . . . he's holding out on you . . . you've got to take matters under your control." He sowed the seed of mistrust in our hearts; he tempted us to seize control.

❧ *Something shifted in our hearts at that moment and we fell from grace. What strikes you about our fall and it's impact upon you?*

❧ *Where in your world has our fall had an effect?*

❧ *Why does life as we know it not come anywhere near the desires we have in our hearts?*

❧ *Our longings for beauty, intimacy, adventure rarely match how life actually unfolds . . . why?*

But wait.

Consider also this: every great story has a rescue.

Jack will come to rescue Rose. William Wallace will rise up to rescue Scotland. Luke Skywalker will rescue the princess and then the free peoples of the universe. Nemo's father rescues him. Nathaniel rescues beautiful Cora—not just once, but twice. Neo breaks the power of the Matrix and sets a captive world free. Aslan comes to rescue Narnia. I could name a thousand more. Why does every great story have a rescue?

❧ *Have you noticed this—that every great story has a rescue? Have you understood our story as one of rescue?*

The challenge God faces is rescuing a people who have no idea how captive they are; no real idea how desperate they are. We know we long for Eden, but we hesitate to give ourselves back to God in abandoned trust. We are captivated by the lies of our Enemy.

❧ *How do we know God's heart for us is good?*

❧ *Does Kierkegaard's parable help explain the gospel?*

The life, death, and resurrection of Jesus of Nazareth answer once and for all the question, "What is God's heart toward me?" At the point of our deepest betrayal, when we had run our farthest from him and gotten so lost we could never find our way home, God came and died to rescue us. You have never been loved like this. He has come to save you in every way a person can be saved. That is God's heart toward you.

❖ *What does your heart do with this realization?*

SOMETHING TO PONDER

❧ *John says, "We are haunted by Eden." What did God intend (again, prior to the Fall) for a woman or a man to be? Do some of the deep, true desires of your heart give you some clues as to what God created you to be? Perhaps a woman's desire to be romanced, to play an irreplaceable role in a shared adventure, and to unveil beauty speaks to God's original intent for a woman. And, for a man, perhaps his desire for a battle to fight, an adventure to live, and a beauty to rescue speaks of God's original intent for a man. What do you believe God intended for you when he created you?*

✦ *How has he begun to restore your true identity?*

THEOLOGY

Creation is a glorious event we all too often rush through, as if it were a brief parenthesis to get to Genesis 3 and the Fall, where we mistakenly think our story really begins. But we must linger on the wonder and beauty of the world and life God intended for us to enjoy, to see the good intentions of his heart for us before we hastily jump to the Fall. Created as Image-bearers, we are designed for a heroic intimacy with God, endowed with a dignity, a freedom, and a glory that made a passionate loving relationship with him possible.

Furthermore, God is a passionate lover who seeks our hearts. As devastating as the Fall was to humanity, God pursued us, inviting us to choose him and the life he offers. He pursues us still! (See Isaiah 54:4–8, 57:7–11, 62:1–5, 62:12; Jeremiah 3:1, 24:7, 31:3–4, 31:31–34.) Notice also the progression of metaphors Jesus uses to teach us about our relationship with him. It moves from clay and potter through sheep and shepherd to bride and bridegroom!

SUPPORTING SCRIPTURE

Darkness over the deep and God's breath hovering over the waters. (Genesis 1:2 *Alter*)

. . . while the morning stars sang together and all the angels shouted for joy. (Job 38:7 NIV)

Then God said, "Let us make a human in our own image, by our likeness, to hold sway over the fish of the sea and the fowl of the heavens and the cattle and the wild beasts and all the crawling thins that crawl upon the earth." And God created the human in his image. (Genesis 1:26–27 *Alter*)

Now the serpent was more crafty than any of the wild animals the LORD God had made. He said to the woman, "Did God really say, 'You must not eat from any tree in the garden'?" The woman said to the serpent, "We may eat fruit from the trees in the garden, but God did say, 'You must not eat fruit from the tree that is in the middle of the garden, and you must not touch it, or you will die.'" "You will not surely die," the serpent said to the woman." For God knows that when you eat of it your eyes will be opened, and you will be like God, knowing good and evil." When the woman saw that the fruit of the tree was good for food and pleasing to the eye, and also desirable for gaining wisdom, she took some and ate it. She also gave some to her husband, who was with her, and he ate it. (Genesis 3:1–6 NIV)

The LORD saw how great man's wickedness on the earth had become, and that every inclination of the thoughts of his heart was only evil all the time. The LORD was grieved that he had made man on the earth, and his heart was filled with pain. (Genesis 6:5–6 NIV)

Above all else, guard your heart, for it is the wellspring of life. (Proverbs 4:23 NIV)

When I look at the night sky and see the work of your fingers—
  the moon and the stars you set in place—
what are mere mortals that you should think about them,
  human beings that you should care for them?
Yet you made them only a little lower than God
  and crowned them with glory and honor. (Psalm 8:3–5 NLT)

The LORD is a warrior . . . (Exodus 15:3 NIV)

I long to be gracious to you. You are precious and honored in my sight, because I love you. But you are the offspring of adulterers. You have made your bed on a high and lofty hill, forsaking me, you uncovered your bed, you climbed into it and opened it wide. You have been false to me. (Excerpts from Isaiah)

I remember the devotion of your youth, how as a bride you loved me . . . What fault did you find in me that you strayed so far from me? You are a swift she-camel running here and there, sniffing the wind in her craving—in her heat who can restrain her? Should I not punish them for this? Should I not avenge myself? I have loved you with an everlasting love; I have drawn you with loving kindness. What have I done to make you hate me so much? (Excerpts from Jeremiah)

I will answer you according to your idols [your false lovers] in order to recapture your heart. (From Ezekiel)

"Their hearts are always going astray . . ." (Hebrews 3:10 NIV)

"As the Father has loved me, so have I loved you. Now remain in my love." (John 15:9 NIV)

"I will give them a heart to know me, that I am the LORD. They will be my people, and I will be their God, for they will return to me with all their heart." (Jeremiah 24:7 NIV)

"... *the Son of Man ... [came] to give his life as a ransom for many.*" (Matthew 20:28 NIV)

For he has rescued us from the dominion of darkness and brought us into the kingdom of the Son he loves, in whom we have redemption, the forgiveness of sins. (Colossians 1:13, 14 NIV)

"*Surely this man was the Son of God!*" (Mark 15:39 NIV)

Act Four

THE KINGDOM RESTORED

See! The winter is past;
the rains are over and gone.
Flowers appear on the earth;
the season of singing has come . . .
—SONG OF SOLOMON 2:11, 12 NIV

And they lived happily ever after.

Stop for just a moment, and let it be true. *They lived happily ever after.* These may be the most beautiful and haunting words in the entire library of mankind.

❧ *Think of the stories that you love. Remember how they "end." Describe a few of your favorite endings.*

◆ *What if? What if this was our ending? What would it be like to have a wild hope rise within you?*

◆ *What would "happily ever after" look like for you?*

You see, every story has an ending. Every story. Including yours. Have you ever faced this? Even if you do manage to find a little taste of Eden in this life, even if you are one of the fortunate souls who finds some love and happiness in the world, you cannot hang on to it. You know this. Your health cannot hold out forever. Age will conquer you. One by one your friends and loved ones will slip from your hand. Your work will remain unfinished. Your time on this stage will come to an end. Like every other person gone before you, you will breathe your last breath.

❧ *And then what? Is that the end of the Story?*

Our enemy is a thief, and one of the things he has stolen from us is the magic, the wonder, the wild hope and joy of the "happily ever after."

❧   *What reason does John give that people drink too much, eat too much, watch too much TV, and basically just check out of life?*

PARADISE REGAINED

Act Four also begins with light, with a dawn, revealing a Paradise.

Only, this Paradise is familiar somehow.

Look at the life of Jesus. Notice what he did. When Jesus

touched the blind, they could *see*; all the beauty of the world opened before them. When he touched the deaf, they were able to *hear*; for the first time in their lives they heard laughter and music and their children's voices. He touched the lame, and they *jumped* to their feet and began to dance. And he called the dead back to *life* and gave them to their families.

Do you see? Wherever humanity was broken, Jesus restored it. He is giving us an illustration here, and there, and there again. The coming of the kingdom of God *restores* the world he made.

◈   *Have you ever connected those ideas to realize that Jesus restores, and that Act Four is a great restoration? What does that stir in you?*

After he laid down his life for us, Jesus of Nazareth was laid in a tomb. He was buried just like any other dead person. His family and friends mourned. His enemies rejoiced. And most of the world went on with business as usual, clueless to the Epic around them. Then, after three days, also at dawn, his story took a sudden and dramatic turn.

Jesus came back. He showed up again. He was restored to them. He walked into the house where they had gathered to comfort one another in their grief and asked if they had anything to eat. It was the most stunning, unbelievable, happiest ending to a story you could possibly imagine.

And it is also ours.

So we, too, shall live and never die. Creation will be restored, and *we* will be restored. And we shall share it together.

✣ *What about heaven do you look forward to? How has your view of heaven changed from reading this chapter?*

✤ *Will everyone enjoy this promise of a happy ending? Why or why not?*

LIFE AT LAST

And life *is* the offer, friends. Let us not forget that.

There is no simpler or more beautiful way to say it than this: Act Four is the restoration of life as it was always meant to be.

It is the return of the beauty, the intimacy, and the adventure we were created to enjoy and have longed for every day of our lives. And yet, *better*, for it is immortal. We can never lose it again. It cannot be taken away. Sunrise and sunset tell the tale every day, remembering Eden's glory, foretelling Eden's return.

❧ *What's the effect of this chapter on you? As you end it, what are you feeling, thinking? Where does all this leave you?*

SOMETHING TO PONDER

❧ *Go back and watch the ending of the stories that you love. Put yourself in the end of the story, and say, "This is my story. This is how life is going to turn out for me very soon." It will do your heart a world of good.*

Continue writing your story by writing out the conclusion . . . how will your story of this life end, and what will heaven hold for you?

❧   *Who in your circle of friends is living without faith? Has a better understanding of the Larger Story given you a different perspective or changed your heart toward these friends? Would hearing Epic give them a new slant on their life, God's heart for them, and the obstacles and sorrows they've faced? Could you share this Larger Story with them? Make a list of those people you want to give a copy of Epic to.*

THEOLOGY

This Act may be the one we know the least about—heaven. Most of us do not live with a deep-rooted excitement about the life to come. It's absolutely amazing how little is taught or preached about heaven. It begins with a party, a feast—more specifically, a wedding reception party beyond what many of us would be comfortable partaking of in this life. (See Revelation 19:6–9, Matthew 26:29, Isaiah 25:6–9).

John challenges a treasured notion in the church, that heaven is unending worship of God. This idea might have been drawn from Revelation 4:8, but note that it is not the saints who "never stop saying: 'Holy, holy, holy,'" but the four creatures, and the twenty-four elders. We know that we are to reign over kingdoms (see Matthew 24:45–46, 25:14–23, 31–34, Luke 19:11–19)—clearly, we are to be about a great deal of activities in the life to come, in addition to worshiping God!

Heaven is the restoration of all that was lost, stolen, or missed in this life. If we're unaware of the life God intended us to live, we live with a minimum of disappointment and unfortunately, hope. We were meant to live a life we haven't fully lived . . . but we will one day. The difficult task with this subject is really beginning to believe that this life *isn't* all there is. We have been so completely blinded to this truth most believers practically do not believe or live as if there is a heaven. On restoration, see Matthew 19:28 and also Revelation 21:1, 5, Isaiah 65:17, and Romans 8:22–23.

SUPPORTING SCRIPTURE

Then I saw a new heaven and a new earth . . . (Revelation 21:1 NIV)

"Behold, I will create new heavens and a new earth." (Isaiah 65:17 NIV)

"I am making everything new!" (Revelation 21:5 NIV)

We know that the whole creation has been groaning as in the pains of childbirth right up to the present time. Not only so, but we ourselves, who have the first fruits of the Spirit, groan inwardly as we wait eagerly for our adoption as sons, the redemption of our bodies. (Romans 8:22–23 NIV)

Very early on the first day of the week, just after sunrise, they were on their way to the tomb and they asked each other, "Who will roll the stone away from the entrance of the tomb?" But when they looked up, they saw that the stone, which was very large, had been rolled away. As they entered the tomb, they saw a young man dressed in a white robe sitting on the right side, and they were alarmed. "Don't be alarmed," he said. "You are looking for Jesus the Nazarene, who was crucified. He has risen! He is not here. See the place where they laid him. But go, tell his disciples . . . 'He is going ahead of you into Galilee. There you will see him, just as he told you.'" (Mark 16:2–7 NIV)

But in fact, Christ has been raised from the dead. He is the first of a great harvest of all who have died. (1 Corinthians 15:20 NLT)

God knew what he was doing from the very beginning. He decided from the outset to shape the lives of those who love him along the same lines as the life of his Son. The Son stands first in the line of humanity he restored. (Romans 8:29 MSG)

"Blessed are those who are invited to the wedding feast of the Lamb." (Revelation 19:9 NLT)

"The kingdom of heaven is like a king who prepared a wedding banquet for his son. He sent his servants to those who had been invited to the banquet to tell them to come, but they refused to come. Then he sent some more servants and said, 'Tell those who have been invited that I have prepared my dinner . . . Come to the wedding banquet.' But they paid no attention and went off—one to his field, another to his business." (Matthew 22:2–5 NIV)

"Mark my words—I will not drink wine again until the day I drink it new with you in my Father's Kingdom." (Matthew 26:29 NLT).

"[The LORD] is patient with you, not wanting anyone to perish, but everyone to come to repentance." (2 Peter 3:9 NIV)

I have set before you life and death . . . Now choose life . . .
(Deuteronomy 30:19 NIV)

". . . come to me to have life." (John 5:40 NIV)

*"The thief comes only to steal and kill and destroy; I have come that
they may have life, and have it to the full."* (John 10:10 NIV)

*"And this is the way to have eternal life—to know you, the only true
God, and Jesus Christ, the one you sent to earth."* (John 17:3 NLT)

*Whoever is thirsty, let him come; and whoever wishes, let him take the
free gift of the water of life.* (Revelation 22:17 NIV)

*"'Come, you who are blessed by my Father; take your inheritance,
the kingdom prepared for you since the creation of the world.'"*
(Matthew 25:34 NIV, emphasis added)

*"Who then is the faithful and wise servant, whom the master has put
in charge of the servants in his household to give them their food at the
proper time? It will be good for that servant whose master finds him
doing so when he returns. I tell you the truth, he will put him in charge
of all his possessions."* (Matthew 24:45–47 NIV)

*The created world itself can hardly wait for what's coming next.
Everything in creation is being more or less held back. God reins it in*

until both creation and all the creatures are ready and can be released at the same moment into the glorious times ahead. (Romans 8: 19–20 MSG)

. . . creation looks forward to the day when it will join God's children in glorious freedom from death and decay. (Romans 8:21 NLT)

"And if I go and prepare a place for you, I will come back and take you to be with me" (John 14:2–3 NIV).

. . . a veil covers their hearts. But whenever anyone turns to the Lord, the veil is taken away. (2 Corinthians 3:15–16 NIV)

We do this by keeping our eyes on Jesus, the champion who initiates and perfects our faith. Because of the joy awaiting him, he endured the cross, disregarding its shame. Now he is seated in the place of honor beside God's throne. (Hebrews 12:2 NLT)

THE ROAD BEFORE US

The Road goes ever on and on
Down from the door where it began.
Now far ahead the Road has gone,
And I must follow, if I can,
Pursuing it with eager feet,
Until it joins some larger way.

—J. R. R TOLKIEN

And now? Now we are living somewhere toward the end of Act Three. We have a future, but this tale is not over yet—not by a long shot. We now live between the battle for Helm's Deep and the Battle of the Pelennor Fields. Between the beaches of Normandy and the end of the war. Between the fall of the Republic and the fall of the Empire. Between Paradise lost and Paradise regained.

We live in a far more dramatic, far more dangerous Story than we ever imagined. The reason we love The Chronicles of Narnia or *Star Wars* or *The Matrix* or The Lord of the Rings is because they are telling us something about our lives that we never, ever get on the evening news. Or from most pulpits. They are reminding us of the Epic we are created for.

❧ *This is the sort of tale you've fallen into. How would you live differently if you believed it to be true?*

Something has been calling to you all the days of your life. You've heard it on the wind and in the music you love, in laughter and in tears, and most especially in the stories that have ever captured your heart. There *is* a secret written on your heart. A valiant Hero-Lover and his Beloved. An Evil One and a great battle to fight. A Journey and a Quest, more dangerous and more thrilling than you could imagine. A little Fellowship to see you through.

This is the gospel of Christianity.

꘎ *How has your understanding of "the gospel of Christianity" changed through reading* Epic?

꘎ *Now—what is your part? What is your role in the Story?*

◆ *To play your part well, you must know your role. What, as a young boy or girl, did you once dream or hope your role would be? (Another way of approaching this question would be to consider the characters you love in Scripture, in the movies, and in your favorite stories. What is it about them, and their story that you would love to believe is true of you?)*

In truth, the only one who can tell you that is the Author. To find our lives, we must turn to Jesus. We must yield our all to him and ask him to restore us as his own. We ask his forgiveness for our betrayal of him. We ask him to make us all he intended us to be— to tell us who we are and what we are now to do. We ask him to remove the veil from our eyes and from our hearts. And may we add that your search might best be helped by a simple prayer,

Jesus, if you really are who you say you are, I ask you to reveal yourself to me. Come, and walk with me so that I might know myself what you are truly like, what your heart is towards me. Open my eyes to the Truth. Open the eyes of my heart to You.

Others of you are ready to enter into a personal relationship with God now. You sense he has been wooing you—through *Epic* and through many things—and you are at the point where you want to open your heart to Jesus Christ as your Rescuer and Restorer. You are ready to come home to God. If this prayer expresses the desires of your heart, well then, simply pray it. Take the plunge.

Jesus, I need you. I need your love. I need the life you offer. I ask you to come and rescue me. Forgive me for living so far from you. I give myself back to you, my Creator and my God. Thank you for giving your life for me, for dying on the cross to pay for all of my sins and to ransom me from the Evil One. I ask you to come into my life as my truest friend and my Savior. Restore me in your Love to be your friend, to live intimately with you. Restore me by your Life to be the person I was always meant to be. I surrender control of my life to you, and I receive your gift of Life.

Now, if that is the cry of your heart and to the best of your knowledge you've prayed that with sincerity, then know this: Jesus has accepted you. You are his now. "Yet to all who received him, to those who believed in his name, he gave the right to become children of God" (John 1:12 NIV). Jesus promised that, "whoever comes to me I will never drive away" (John 6:37 NIV), and "I stand at the door and knock. If anyone hears my voice and opens the door [of your heart to me], I will come in" (Revelation 3:20 NIV). He has come in to your heart.

Your journey has just taken the dramatic turn. You have been rescued from the kingdom of Darkness and transferred to the kingdom of Jesus Christ, the kingdom of God. You have passed from death to life. Congratulations! The angels are cheering! We rejoice with you!

Now, in all fairness, we must say: Be prepared. The Evil One does not lose his captives gladly. Sometimes, life can get harder before it gets better. You have taken sides in the great Battle. You are now a dangerous person, an ally of the true King operating behind enemy lines. Your first battle now is to grow close to God and to his friends.

<ul><li>The Story God is telling—like every great story—reminds us of three eternal truths it would be good to keep in mind. Summarize your thoughts on what John describes as the Three Eternal Truths:</li></ul>

Things are not what they seem.

We are at war.

You have a crucial role to play.

We are now far into this Epic that every great story points to. We have reached the moment where we, too, must find our courage and rise up to recover our hearts and fight for the hearts of others. The hour is late, and much time has been wasted.

Jesus calls to you to be his intimate ally once more. There are great things to be done and great sacrifices to be made. You won't lose heart if you know what's really going on here, where this Story is headed and what your Lover has promised to you.

This is the gospel.

This is the Story we are living in.

May you play your part well.

⚘ *What do you think the lasting impact of going through Epic is?*

❧   *What will change in the way you live?*

❧   *Who do you want to share this with?*

Something to Ponder

❧   *Below, write a prayer, asking God to reveal to you your true name, your true identity from God that will give clarity to your life purpose and calling. (It might help to read "Finding Your Role" on* www.epicreality.com.)

Now that you've become aware of the power of a person's story, begin to ask those closest to you to share their story with you. Take an hour or two just to listen and ask questions of your friend's story (those in your Bible study, small group, or Sunday school fellowship). It will change how you see them, understand them, and relate to them.

And continue to look at your life as a story within a much larger story. As you journal and pray and reflect upon you life, continue to piece together your story, your role, the assaults of the enemy, and the goodness of God toward you. In other words, don't forget your story!

John wrote *Epic* as a way for us to share the gospel with those who don't yet know Christ. Who can you give this Story to? You could buy them the book, or take them through the DVD, or start by going to an epic movie together and talking about the similarities to Christianity! (For ideas on how to share this Epic God is telling, see www.epicreality.com, especially "Share the Story".)

THEOLOGY

We live in a Larger Story. That should be clear by now.

Things are not what they seem. The snake in the Garden was more than a snake! The carpenter from Nazareth was more than a woodworker! (See 2 Corinthians 4:18.)

We are at war. Yes, it's a love story . . . set in a life or death battle. Satan is seeking to steal, kill, destroy. Jesus is bringing us life. (See John 10:10.)

You have a crucial role to play. (See John 15:15–17, 17:18, Ephesians 2:10).

SUPPORTING SCRIPTURE

. . . a veil covers their hearts. But whenever anyone turns to the Lord, the veil is taken away. (2 Corinthians 3:15–16 NIV)

We do this by keeping our eyes on Jesus, the champion who initiates and perfects our faith. Because of the joy awaiting him, he endured the cross, disregarding its shame. Now he is seated in the place of honor beside God's throne. (Hebrews 12:2 NLT)

READY FOR MORE?

A good next step in your heart's journey would be to read your way through the articles on www.epicreality.com and then visit www.ransomedheart.com, John Eldredge's Web site.

There you will find lots more audio, video, and book resources, live events and a community forum, which can aid you along the way.

———————◄►———————

John Eldredge is an author and teacher. Some of his other books are *Waking the Dead, Wild at Heart, The Sacred Romance, The Journey of Desire,* and *Captivating* (with his wife, Stasi). John lives in Colorado with Stasi and their three sons.

You can learn more about John's work at: www.epicreality.com.

Bible Translations Quoted From

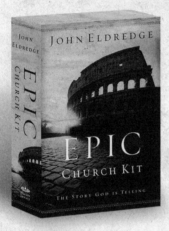

YOU WERE BORN INTO AN
EPIC ... DISCOVER IT.

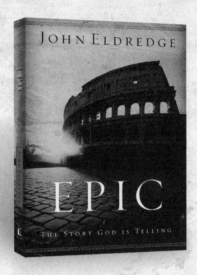

IN **EPIC**, A RETELLING OF THE GOSPEL IN four acts, John Eldredge invites us to revisit the drama of life, viewing God not only as the author but also as the lead actor, exploring His motives and His heart. Eldredge examines the power of story, the universal longing for a "plot" that makes sense deep inside us, our desire for a meaningful role to play, our love of books and movies, and how all of this points us to the gospel itself.

This title is also available in packs of 10.

For more information, check out http://www.thomasnelson.com/epic
or call 1-800-933-9673